A HISTORICAL ALBUM OF

COLORADO

A HISTORICAL ALBUM OF

COLORADO

Charles A. Wills

THE MILLBROOK PRESS, Brookfield, Connecticut

Front and back cover: "The Rocky Mountains, Long's Peak." Painting by Albert Bierstadt, 1877. Denver Public Library, Western History Department.

Title page: Rocky Mountain National Park. Courtesy of the Boulder Convention & Visitors Bureau.

Library of Congress Cataloging-in-Publication Data

Wills, Charles A.
    A historical album of Colorado / Charles A. Wills.
        p. cm. – (Historical Albums)
    Includes bibliographical references and index.
    Summary: A history of Colorado, from its early exploration and
settlement to the state today.
      ISBN 1-56294-592-0 (lib. bdg.) ISBN 1-56294-858-X (tr. pbk.)
      1. Colorado—History—Juvenile literature. 2. Colorado—
Gazetteers—Juvenile literature. I. Title. II. Series.
F776.3.W55 1996
978.8—dc20   95-40417
                                       CIP
                                       AC

 Created in association with Media Projects Incorporated

C. Carter Smith, *Executive Editor*
Kimberly Horstman, *Project Editor*
Charles A. Wills, *Principal Writer*
Bernard Schleifer, *Art Director*
John W. Kern, *Production Editor*
Arlene Goldberg, *Cartographer*

Consultant: Dr. Marilynn Jo Hitchens, Teacher,
Wheat Ridge High School, Denver, Colorado

Manufactured in the United States of America

10 9 8 7 6 5 4 3 2 1

CONTENTS

Introduction

Colorado has always held a special place in America's imagination.

First, there is the state's dazzling landscape, dominated by the Rocky Mountains. "Little in the world can compare" with Colorado, wrote a journalist many years ago. "The vistas stretch the eyes, enlighten the heart, and make the spirit humble." On a visit early in the 20th century, President Theodore Roosevelt said, "The scenery bankrupts the English language."

Then there is Colorado's extraordinary mineral wealth. Tales of gold lured the first Spanish explorers to the region more than five centuries ago, and while they failed to find what they were looking for, later arrivals were luckier. From the Pikes Peak gold rush of 1858 to the uranium boom of the 1950s, the quest for mineral riches has lured people to Colorado.

Colorado's history, however, is much more than tales of mountains and minerals. It is the story of great Native American cultures, from the ancient civilization at Mesa Verde to the buffalo-hunting warriors who roamed the state's eastern grasslands; of farmers struggling to turn Colorado's dry plains into green crop land; of great engineering projects to bring roads and water through the mountains.

Colorado's history is also a story with much conflict—decades of bitter warfare between white settlers and Native Americans in the 19th century, labor clashes in the early part of the 20th century, and now the important struggle to balance the state's amazing growth against the need to preserve its environment.

Together, these different strands combine to tell the story of one of America's most beautiful, vibrant, and exciting states.

PART ONE

A DIVERSE PAST

This view of the Mount of the Holy Cross near Vail was painted by 19th-century artist Thomas Moran. A peak of the Sawatch Range, the mountain has two clefts that intersect at right angles; when the snows melt each spring, the clefts remain filled with snow, creating a white cross that is visible for many miles.

Before the arrival of the first Spanish explorers in the 16th century, Colorado was home to several Native American cultures, from the cliff-dwelling Anasazis of Mesa Verde in the west to the buffalo-hunting tribes of the eastern plains. As a Spanish territory (although claimed for years by France), most of Colorado came under American rule with the Louisiana Purchase of 1803; the rest was won from Mexico in the Mexican-American War forty years later. The early decades of the 19th century saw increased exploration and the first settlements in Colorado, but the region's development was slow until gold was discovered in the 1850s. With its population swelled by tens of thousands of fortune hunters, Colorado became a territory in 1861.

Native Americans of Pueblos and Plains

Colorado's natural history began half a billion years ago, when inland North America was the floor of a great ocean. Over hundreds of millions of years, the water drained away and the mighty Rocky Mountain chain thrust itself upward.

The Rocky Mountains are Colorado's greatest natural feature. Running north-south, they split the landscape of the modern-day state into eastern and western slopes. The Rockies also form the Continental Divide—the line from which waterways flow either east toward the Mississippi-Missouri river system and the Gulf of Mexico, or west toward the Pacific Ocean.

Many individual mountain ranges make up the Rocky Mountains—the Park Range, the Sawatch Mountains, the San Juan Range, and many others. These mountain ranges make Colorado America's highest state, with an average elevation (height above sea level) of nearly 6,800 feet, or well over a mile. Fifty-three mountains of 14,000 feet or higher can be found within the state's 104,000 square miles.

But not all of Colorado is mountainous. In the eastern half of the state, the land is part of the Great Plains region—flat, dry, almost treeless grasslands that stretch eastward from the Rockies. Beyond the western slope of the Rockies, the landscape is made up of valleys and mesas. (A mesa is a hill with a flat top; the term, used by early Spanish explorers, comes from the Spanish word for table.)

Colorado's human story starts about 15,000 years ago, when the first people arrived in the region. These first Coloradoans were the descendants of Asian peoples who, it is thought, had walked to North America from Asia across a strip of land that once linked the two continents at the Bering Straight.

Only a few fragments of bone and stone tools remain to tell us how these people lived, but the original Coloradoans were certainly a nomadic (wandering) people who moved from place to place in search of animals to hunt.

Between 1,400 and 2,000 years ago, these nomadic hunters began to settle permanently in caves among the mesas of southwestern Colorado. They planted crops—the most important being corn—and wove containers and sandals from plant fibers such as straw and vines. Archaeologists (historians of the ancient past) have named these people the Basket Maker Culture. Those that lived at Mesa Verde, in the southwestern region of present-

Cliff Palace, the largest of the Anasazi dwellings at Mesa Verde, contains more than 200 rooms and probably housed about 250 people. The circular structures are the remains of kivas, underground chambers where religious ceremonies were held.

day Colorado, became known as the Anasazis ("Ancient Ones").

Over the centuries, the Anasazis developed into one of North America's most remarkable Indian civilizations. The cave dwellings at Mesa Verde gave way to "pit houses"—dugouts with roofs and walls made of wood—and finally to pueblos (towns), cut into the rocky walls of the mesa itself. These pueblos were similar to modern-day apartment houses, with family dwellings stacked several stories high, complete with terraces and shafts to bring air and sunlight indoors.

On top of the mesas and in the valleys below, the Anasazis grew corn, beans, and pumpkins. The fiber of the yucca plant provided thread for clothing, which was decorated with feathers and precious stones. In a region with little rainfall, the Anasazis dammed streams and dug reservoirs to hold water for their crops. Their elaborately painted pottery was among the most beautiful made by Native Americans.

By A.D. 1000, the Anasazis abandoned their mesa-top villages, preferring instead to build their pueblos on cliff ledges. These dwellings provided better protection against invaders and weather conditions.

And then, in a single generation, the Mesa Verde civilization disappeared. The reason for the Anasazis' decline still isn't clear, but it was probably caused by a drought that hit the region between A.D. 1275–1300. Without water their crops failed and the people of Mesa Verde were forced to leave their pueblos and migrate into what is now northern Arizona and New Mexico. Mesa Verde was abandoned and forgotten until 1888, when two ranchers out for a ride found the remains of this lost civilization.

The Anasazis were not the only Native American culture to develop in Colorado. The Utes—"People of the Blue Sky" in their own language—lived on the western slope of the Rocky Mountains and spread into other parts of the region. Divided into four separate groups and many smaller clans, the Utes were a nomadic people who lived by hunting buffalo.

The buffalo was also the mainstay of the Native American groups who roamed across Colorado's eastern grasslands. These groups included the Cheyennes, the Arapahoes, the Dakotas (or Sioux), the Pawnees, and the Comanches.

The buffalo, found in huge herds across the Great Plains, provided not only food but hides for clothing and shelter and bone for tools. Hunting the buffalo, however, was a dangerous business. Usually, Native American hunters tried to stampede buffalo herds over cliffs rather than approach the huge animals on foot armed with just a bow and arrow.

In the late 17th and 18th centuries, the arrival of the horse changed the lives of the Great Plains People forever. Although horses were first brought to North America by Spanish colonists from the south, the Great Plains tribes probably obtained their first horses from another Native American group, the Apaches, who often raided Spanish settlements.

Horses gave the Plains Indians greater mobility: Now hunters could easily follow the buffalo herds on horseback. Because they could also carry many of their possessions, like portable tepee poles and buffalo hides for shelter, the Native Americans were able to stay away from their villages for much longer and follow the herds farther. Hunting buffalo on horseback also greatly reduced the chance of being trampled.

The arrival of the horse led to a golden age for the Great Plains tribes which would last until the first white settlers pushed their way into the region in the mid-1800s.

This engraving shows Plains Indians on the move, transporting their possessions on a travois—a triangular frame of wooden poles covered with buffalo rawhide, which was usually lashed to a horse or dog. When the travelers stopped for the evening, the poles and buffalo skins were used to construct a tepee.

Life for the Cheyennes and Arapahoes revolved around the summertime buffalo hunt, when individual villages joined forces to pursue the great "southern herd" that grazed along the Platte River. This 19th-century painting by William Henry Jackson shows Indians driving a herd of buffalo over a cliff—a hunting technique that often provided tribes with enough meat to last through a long winter.

Spain and France in the Southwest

Spain was the first European nation to stake a claim to the land that became Colorado. Starting with Christopher Columbus's first voyage to what Europeans called the New World in 1492, Spain took the lead in exploring and settling the Americas. By the mid-1500s, the Spanish empire in North America included Florida and Mexico, and Spanish *conquistadors* (conquerors) began to move deeper into the continent in search of riches and to convert the Indians to Christianity.

Rumors of gold-rich lands north of Mexico eventually reached Spain's king, Charles I. In 1540, the king or-

Wearing armor and carrying lances and harquebuses (early firearms), Coronado and his men march across desert terrain during the great expedition of 1540–42 in this painting by Frederic Remington.

dered the governor of the Mexican province of Nueva Galicia, Francisco Vásquez de Coronado, to lead an expedition to investigate these tales.

The entrada (expedition) numbered 2,000 men, including Spanish soldiers and priests and many Mexican Indians, plus great herds of cattle, sheep, and horses. For nearly two years the expedition traveled across 3,000 miles of plains, deserts, and mountains, from present-day Arizona to Kansas.

At one point in the journey, Coronado, or one of his officers, may have crossed Colorado's southeastern corner; modern historians aren't sure. The expedition was one of history's greatest explorations, but it ended in disappointment for its leader. Coronado never found the riches he sought, and he wrote to the king, ". . . And what I am sure of is that there is not any gold nor any other metal in all that country." But Coronado was wrong. Hundreds of years later, great deposits of gold, silver, and other minerals would lure thousands of fortune hunters to Colorado.

Coronado's journey gave the Spanish the basis for their claim to the North American Southwest, but for the next fifty years they left the region to the buffalo and to the Native Americans. At the close of the 16th century, however, rumors of gold again reached Spain. This time, the Spanish government organized the region into the province of New Mexico, with Juan de Oñate as its governor.

In 1598, Oñate led 400 colonists north into present-day New Mexico. After founding a settlement called San Juan, the governor traveled north to look for gold. Oñate and his companions reached the San Luis Valley, thus becoming the first Europeans known to have set foot in what is now Colorado. Oñate traveled as far as the site of present-day Denver, but like Coronado before him he found no gold.

Meanwhile another European nation, France, began to take an interest in the Southwest. In 1682, Robert Cavalier, Sieur de La Salle, journeyed down the Mississippi River and claimed all the land drained by the river for France. This territory, which La Salle named Louisiana for France's King Louis XIV, overlapped much of the land claimed by Spain, including Colorado.

In 1706, a Spanish soldier named Juan de Ulibarri led an expedition into Colorado, following a group of Picuríe Indians from Taos Pueblo in present-day New Mexico. He claimed that the Picuríes had been kidnapped by the Apaches, but they may have been fleeing Spanish rule, which was often cruel.

Ulibarri found the Picuríes living among the Apaches at a village he called El Cuartelejo in what is now eastern Colorado. The Apaches gave up their captives (if they were indeed captives), but Ulibarri was shocked to see that the Apaches carried French-made guns. Eager to strengthen Spain's claim to the area, he had the Apache leaders swear an oath of loyalty to Spain's King Philip V.

Over the next few decades, Spanish soldiers and missionaries occasionally journeyed into Colorado. Although the Spanish didn't establish any permanent colonies in the region, they explored much of it, finding and naming many of the places, such as the Sangre de Cristo (Blood of Christ) Mountains. The state's name, Colorado, actually comes from the Spanish word for reddish, the color of the region's rivers as a result of deposits of soil and minerals in the water.

The greatest Spanish exploration came in 1776, the same year rebels in the British colonies far to the east declared their independence and founded the United States of America. Two priests, Padre (Father) Silvestre Vélez de Escalante and Fray (Brother) Antanasio Domínguez, set out to find a route between Santa Fe, the capital of New Mexico, and the Spanish missions (religious settlements) on the California coast.

The Sierra Nevadas kept Escalante and Domínguez from reaching California, but in a journey filled with hardship and hunger they explored and mapped a huge stretch of land, including much of western Colorado. Their journey lasted five months and covered nearly 1,800 miles. In the words of a later historian, "[Escalante and Domínguez] made one of the most notable explorations in North American history. . . . They explored more unknown territory than Daniel Boone, George Rogers Clark, or even Lewis and Clark."

Drawn from the reports of Escalante and Domínguez, this Spanish map shows the territory between the Rockies and the Sierra Nevadas on the Pacific Coast. Despite its many inaccuracies, it was the first map of the region based on eyewitness accounts.

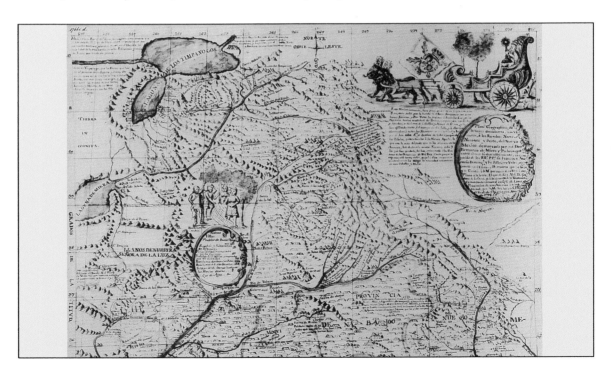

The Explorers

Despite La Salle's claims, France did little to explore and nothing to colonize the Southwest. In 1763, France gave up its claims to territory west of the Mississippi. That situation changed suddenly in 1801, when France's dictator, Napoleon Bonaparte, secretly forced Spain to put the vast Louisiana Territory back under French rule.

This arrangement lasted just two years: In 1803, Napoleon, needing cash, sold the entire Louisiana Territory to the United States for nearly $15 million. This "Louisiana Purchase" doubled the size of the young United States, and among the land gained was all of Colorado east of the Continental Divide—roughly the eastern half of the present state.

Eager to find out what this huge and mostly unexplored territory contained, President Thomas Jefferson authorized two exploring expeditions. The first, led by Meriwether Lewis and William Clark, explored the northern part of the purchase all the way to the Pacific Coast. The second, command-

New Jersey-born army officer Zebulon Pike was already an experienced explorer when he set out across the Plains with twenty-two men in July 1806. Six years after returning from the Rockies, Pike was killed in action against the British during the War of 1812. Shown here is the frontispiece (top) and title page (right) of the 1805–1807 expedition account.

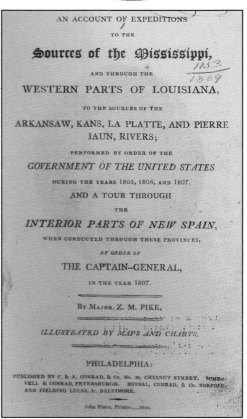

AN ACCOUNT OF EXPEDITIONS

TO THE

Sources of the Mississippi,

AND THROUGH THE

WESTERN PARTS OF LOUISIANA,

TO THE SOURCES OF THE

ARKANSAW, KANS, LA PLATTE, AND PIERRE JAUN, RIVERS;

PERFORMED BY ORDER OF THE

GOVERNMENT OF THE UNITED STATES

DURING THE YEARS 1805, 1806, AND 1807.

AND A TOUR THROUGH

THE

INTERIOR PARTS OF NEW SPAIN,

WHEN CONDUCTED THROUGH THESE PROVINCES,

BY ORDER OF

THE CAPTAIN-GENERAL,

IN THE YEAR 1807.

BY MAJOR Z. M. PIKE.

ILLUSTRATED BY MAPS AND CHARTS.

PHILADELPHIA.

PUBLISHED BY C. & A. CONRAD, & Co. No. 30, CHESNUT STREET. SOMERVELL & CONRAD, PETERSBURGH. BONSAL, CONRAD, & Co. NORFOLK. AND FIELDING LUCAS, Jr. BALTIMORE.

John Binns, Printer....1810.

ed by twenty-seven-year-old Lieutenant Zebulon Pike of the U.S. Army, set out from St. Louis, Missouri, in 1806 to explore the southern part.

Pike and his men crossed present-day Kansas and followed the Arkansas River into eastern Colorado as far as the site of the present-day city of Pueblo. Along the way Pike saw the mountain that remains known as Pikes Peak, although he never actually climbed the 14,100-foot summit.

Then things started to go wrong.

Army engineer Stephen Long led many exploring and surveying expeditions through western territory. On his 1819–20 journey to the Rocky Mountains, Long climbed many mountains, including one, Long's Peak, which he named after himself.

The explorers became lost. Snowstorms, high winds, and hunger added to their misery. Finally they stumbled across the Sangre de Cristo Mountains—only to be arrested by Spanish troops along the Rio Grande.

The Spanish disagreed with the U.S. government over which river formed the Louisiana Territory's southeastern border. Spain's colonial authorities in Santa Fe believed Pike was trespassing on their territory and accused him of spying. Pike and his men were later released and made their way home.

In 1819, the American and Spanish governments reached an agreement settling the border dispute, and another army officer, Major Stephen Long, led an expedition into Colorado. Two members of the expedition managed to climb Pike's Peak, but Long found eastern Colorado's grasslands a disappointment. In his report, Long called the region a "desert" and declared it unfit for American settlement.

Despite Long's gloomy report, the Spanish at Santa Fe expected an American invasion of Colorado. In 1820, Spanish troops built a fort near present-day Walsenburg. Just a year later, however, Mexico achieved independence from Spain. The new Mexican government took control of Spain's southwestern territories, including the parts of Colorado lying south of the Rio Grande and west of the Continental Divide.

The Mountain Men

Escalante and Domínguez, Long, and Pike had all done much to explore Colorado's plains, mountains, and valleys. But the people who did the most to open up the region were not missionary priests or soldiers; they were traders and trappers—the legendary "mountain men."

In the early 1800s, no fashionable gentleman in America or Europe considered himself fully dressed without a tall hat made from the glossy fur of the beaver. This fashion craze made beaver pelts (furs) very valuable and led scores of tough young men to

Two mountain men bait beaver traps in a cold Rocky Mountain lake. The traps were smeared with castoreum, a strong-smelling substance obtained from the beaver's scent gland, and placed just under the water's surface. Lured by the scent, a beaver would become entangled in the trap.

make the difficult journey across the plains and into the Rockies, where large numbers of beavers lived in the cold mountain streams.

Every spring, mountain men set out from St. Louis, Missouri, either alone or in small groups. They were most often French Canadians, Americans, Britons, or many men of mixed white-Native American ancestry. They usually carried little more than a rifle, gunpowder, and lead to make bullets, although large parties brought goods such as tools, whiskey, and guns to trade for furs with Native Americans.

After a long, lonely year in the mountains, a mountain man might return to St. Louis paddling a canoe full of pelts, or else head to the Green River in present-day Wyoming for the Rendezvous, the rowdy annual meeting between trappers and buyers from the great St. Louis fur-trading companies. Many historians believe, however, that half of all mountain men never returned from the Rockies, where they died of hardship or were killed in fights with Native Americans.

The era of the mountain men lasted into the 1830s, when beaver hats fell out of fashion and the over-hunted animals began to disappear. Buffalo-fur robes were now in demand, and hunters and traders invaded eastern Colorado's grasslands in search of great herds of buffalo.

The trade in buffalo hides led to the building of the first real non-Native American outpost in Colorado—Bent's Fort. Built between 1828 and 1832 by William and Charles Bent, the adobe-walled trading post stood on the Arkansas River near what is now the town of La Junta.

For two decades, Bent's Fort was the crossroads of the Southwest—a place where Native Americans, traders, trappers, travelers, and military men met to do business, stock up on supplies, and socialize. Bent's Fort was also a stopping place on a branch of the famous Santa Fe Trail, the trade route connecting St. Louis with Santa Fe, capital of the Mexican southwest.

In the first decades of the 19th century, most Americans were happy to leave the Southwest to the Native Americans and the mountain men. The region was considered a desert, rich in furs but not a promising area for settlement. This view changed in the 1840s, when the idea of Manifest Destiny began to gain a following. This was the belief that the United States had the right—some said the duty—to extend its territory clear across the continent to the Pacific Ocean.

This hunger for land led to conflict with Mexico, the other major power in the West. The United States was the victor in the Mexican-American War of 1846–48, and in the peace treaty that settled the conflict, Mexico gave up its western territory between the Rio Grande and the Pacific Ocean. The stars and stripes now flew over all the land that would become the state of Colorado.

This engraving, published in *Harper's Weekly*, shows a rugged mountain man outfitted for many long months on the trail. Besides trapping beavers, the mountain man spent his days hunting buffalo, moose, and cougar, and fighting off attacks by bears and hostile Native Americans. Although some trappers worked in pairs, for many it was often a lonely, solitary life.

The Colorado Gold Rush

Before 1850, Colorado as we know it today still didn't exist. The 1848 treaty split the present-day state between the Kansas, New Mexico, and Utah territories. The state of Texas also claimed a large portion of the region, but in the Compromise of 1850—a political compromise aimed at cooling the growing conflict between the Northern and Southern states—the federal government bought this land from Texas.

The Colorado region in 1850 was still a remote, unsettled place where Native American tribes followed the buffalo herds, fought battles against one another, and lived as they had for generations.

There were no permanent settlements in Colorado; the only whites in the region were trappers, traders, fortune seekers passing through on the way to the gold fields of California, and an occasional party of soldiers or explorers. Even this small white presence, however, had begun to change the lives of Colorado's Native Americans.

Contact with whites brought useful things to the Cheyennes, Arapahoes, and other Indian nations—guns, for example, which made hunting buffalo even easier. But the whites also brought less welcome things, like disease. The Plains Peoples had no resistance to illnesses like smallpox and measles, and epidemics often killed entire villages. White traders also brought alcohol, something the Native Americans had never before encountered, and for some villages drunkenness proved as deadly as disease.

In 1851, government officials held a council meeting with leaders of the Dakota, Cheyenne, Arapaho, and other Plains Indian nations at Fort Laramie in the Wyoming Territory. Out of this meeting came the Fort Laramie Treaty. Under its terms, the land between the South Platte and Arkansas rivers (including a big stretch of present-day Colorado) was promised to the Cheyennes and Arapahoes "for as long as the grass shall grow and the river shall run."

The year 1851 also saw the founding of the first permanent non-Native American settlement in Colorado. This was the town of San Luis on the Culebra River; its settlers were Mexican-American families from Taos and Santa Fe in New Mexico. Other settlements at Garcia and Conejos followed over the next couple of years. The U.S. Army built two outposts, Fort Massachusetts and Fort Garland, to protect the small farming

villages from attack by local Utes. The conflict with the Utes was just the beginning of decades of bitter fighting between settlers and Native Americans in Colorado.

In 1858, an event took place that changed Colorado history forever. In that year, three brothers from Georgia—Oliver, Levi, and William Russell—arrived in the Pikes Peak region after an exhausting journey. The Russells had heard immigrants returning from California describe traces of gold in the streams around the mountain. Also, William Russell's wife, a Cherokee, had relatives who told stories of gold in the Front Range of the Rocky Mountains.

Fort Massachusetts, a U.S. Army outpost, was built in 1852 along Ute Creek in the San Luis Valley. The fort consisted of several buildings of adobe (sun-dried clay) surrounding a parade field. The fort was abandoned after a second post, Fort Garland, was built six years later.

Traveling photographers reached the Pikes Peak diggings not long after the first miners. Here (left), a confident-looking miner poses for his portrait—perhaps to send to the folks back East. The pick and shovel are props; the chief mining method was panning—swirling soil from a creek bed in a pan to separate gold from gravel.

Very few prospectors who set out for the Pikes Peak gold diggings actually made it. In this grim print (below), an unlucky fortune hunter lies dead, probably from hunger and thirst, alone on the Great Plains.

In July, William Russell found flecks of gold on the bottom of Cherry Creek, a tributary of the South Platte River sixty miles north of Pikes Peak. It wasn't much, but it was enough to inspire hundreds of gold-hungry prospectors to make the long trip west.

Wagons with "Pikes Peak or Bust" painted on their sides soon began lumbering across the plains toward Cherry Creek. For many prospectors, the journey west was a long and hazardous one. Often wagons got lost or broke down on the prairie. Many emigrants perished of thirst, hunger, or disease. In addition, they were very often attacked by Plains Indians who were angry at the prospectors' presence on Native American hunting grounds.

Almost all of the fortune hunters that made it to the Colorado region "busted;" there just wasn't much gold along Cherry Creek. "I have had three days' experience in gold digging," one disappointed prospector wrote home. "The first didn't reach the [golden] color, though I washed a thousand panfuls. The second day about the same number with a shade of yellow dirt, which inspired courage. Third day, near as I can judge . . . I secured about the sixteenth part of a new cent's worth of the genuine article."

One of these prospectors was a Kansan named William Larimer, who established a town that he named Denver after James Denver, governor of the Kansas Territory. This ramshackle community of miners' shacks and tents would grow into Colorado's biggest city and state capital.

The Cherry Creek gold rush soon fizzled out, but in May 1859 prospectors found bigger gold deposits at Gregory Gulch, near Clear Creek, to the south of the "diggings" at Denver.

This strike, plus several others that summer, touched off a huge gold rush that rivaled the one that had swept California a decade before. Americans called the hoards of fortune seekers heading west to Colorado "Fifty-niners" in the same way those who hurried to cash in on the earlier gold rush were known as "Forty-niners." The boom continued in 1860 when still more gold was found at Leadville.

Henry Villard, a German-born newspaper reporter who covered the Clear Creek gold rush, wrote much later that "Not less than fifty to sixty thousand fortune hunters reached the Rocky Mountains before the first of September [1859]. . . . Before the next winter set in the greater part of the territory now included in the boundaries of the state of Colorado had been journeyed and worked over, and in many places permanent mining camps established."

Once Denver merged with the neighboring mining camp of Auraria, it became the capital of gold country.

By 1860 Denver had a population of more than 60,000.

Although a handful of miners did find fortunes along Clear Creek or in the other diggings, most returned home broke, exhausted, and disappointed. But some men decided to stay, and the rough mining camps began to turn into real towns as families arrived from back East. Together with the Mexican-American settlers who had arrived in the San Luis Valley a few years before, these people were the human foundation of the future state of Colorado.

The human wave that swept into Colorado between 1858 and 1861 made some form of government nec-

essary. At first, settlers organized themselves as the "Territory of Jefferson." Then, on February 28, 1861, Congress officially established the Colorado Territory from a rectangular piece of land taken from the neighboring territories of Kansas, Nebraska, New Mexico, and Utah.

Colorado City was the first territorial capital, but in 1862 the territorial legislature moved to Golden, and then in 1867 to Denver, which has remained Colorado's capital ever since.

Years of Conflict

Colorado's first territorial governor, William Gilpin, faced a major crisis as he took office. Just two months after the Colorado Territory was established, the Civil War began when the slaveholding states in South left the Union to form the Confederate States of America.

Governor Gilpin worried that gold-rich Colorado would be too tempting a prize for the Confederacy to ignore. He was right. A Confederate force led by General Henry Sibley was soon marching north from Texas toward Denver. Gilpin recruited pro-Union miners and settlers and led them south through Raton Pass to head off the Confederate advance. Once in the New Mexico Territory, "Gilpin's Pet Lambs of Colorado," as the ragtag army was nicknamed, joined forces with army troops from Fort Union.

On March 27–28, 1862, the Union and Confederate forces, numbering about 1,700 men on both sides, clashed in a two-day battle fought in a snowstorm at La Glorieta Pass in New Mexico. The Confederates held off Gilpin's men, but a small group of Union troops managed to sneak into the Confederate rear and destroy their supplies. Sibley realized he couldn't advance any farther without these supplies and retreated. Gilpin's quick actions had saved Colorado from Confederate occupation.

At the same time, a more brutal conflict was brewing back in the Colorado Territory—this one between whites and Native Americans. Most of the soldiers in the territory had gone to fight the Confederacy in the East. With no troops to stop them, Native Americans grew bold and began attacking isolated ranches and farms and raiding wagon trains.

The Cheyennes and Arapahoes had reason to be angry. The Leadville gold strike had brought many whites into their homeland—a territory guaranteed to them by the Fort Laramie Treaty of 1851. The federal government broke this treaty by allowing settlement in the area, but the Indians were promised money and trade goods in return. These were rarely delivered, however—the government was too busy fighting the Confederacy to care about what was happening to the region's Native Americans.

By 1863, Indian warriors were raiding settlements near Denver. Terrified by the attacks, the territory's white citizens called for action in the harshest words possible. "A few months of active extermination against the red devils," stated an editorial in Denver's *Rocky Mountain News*, "will bring quiet and nothing else will."

The real tragedy was that many Cheyenne and Arapahoe leaders wanted only to reach a peaceful settlement with the whites. The massacres that angered white settlers were mostly the work of a few hotheaded warriors.

This mattered little to the frightened citizens of Denver. They were grateful when John M. Chivington, a Methodist minister and an officer in the territorial militia, led a regiment of volunteers against the Cheyennes.

On the morning of November 29, 1864, Chivington and his men descended upon a Cheyenne village along Sand Creek. The village's chief, Black Kettle, was one of the Cheyenne leaders who wanted to cooperate with the whites. In fact, the U.S. flag flew over the village as a sign of peaceful intentions. It did no good.

What happened on that cold November morning is one of the most tragic and shameful incidents in American history. The Colorado troops swept down on the Native American village and shot, stabbed, and clubbed its people—at least two-thirds of them unarmed women and children—in a frenzy of bloodshed.

It is unknown how many Native Americans died; estimates run between 200 and 500 people. "The slaughter was continuous," an eyewitness said later. "No Indian, old or young, male or female, was spared." Chivington's men then mutilated the bodies of the dead and brought many scalps back to Denver, where they were put on public display.

Chivington became an overnight hero to many Coloradoans, but news of the Sand Creek Massacre shocked many other Americans. Congress eventually investigated the incident

The 1st and 3rd Colorado Volunteers storm Cheyennes' tepees along Sand Creek. Black Kettle, chief of the village, survived the Sand Creek Massacre, only to die four years later in a similar attack at the Washita River in present-day Oklahoma.

and found Chivington guilty of leading a "foul and dastardly massacre."

After the Civil War ended in April 1865, the U.S. Army returned to Colorado and began a relentless campaign against those Cheyennes and Arapahoes who remained on the warpath. By 1867 most of these people had been sent to reservations in Indian Territory (present-day Oklahoma).

Even this didn't destroy the Indians' determination to save their land. In 1868, one thousand Cheyenne, Sioux, and Arapahoe warriors came close to winning a victory over the army when they trapped fifty troops on Beecher Island in the Arikaree River near present-day Wray. For nine days the Native Americans attacked the island, but the troops held them off until reinforcements arrived.

One year later, soldiers killed Tall Bull, the last of the Cheyenne war chiefs, in a fight at Summit Springs. This battle was one of the last clashes between whites and Native Americans on Colorado's eastern plains.

"I have come to kill Indians," Colonel John M. Chivington (top) is reported to have said before the Sand Creek Massacre, "and believe it is right and honorable to use any means under God's heaven to kill Indians."

In this painting (left), army scouts hold off Cheyenne warriors led by the great war chief Roman Nose in September 1869. Whites called the fight "the Battle of Beecher Island," after Lt. Frederick Beecher, who died there; Roman Nose also lost his life in the battle.

PART TWO

THE CENTENNIAL STATE

"Cowboy artist" Charles M. Russell painted this view of life on the trail. By the end of the 1870s, cowboys had brought more than 800,000 head of longhorn cattle from Texas to fatten on the Colorado grasslands.

With the end of the Civil War and the coming of the railroads, more settlers poured into the territory, which finally achieved statehood in 1876. The hunt for mineral wealth continued into the 20th century, fueled by discoveries of more gold and silver plus lesser minerals like lead and coal. In addition, Colorado became an important agricultural and industrial state. The terrible depression years of the 1930s were followed by a wartime boom. In the years since World War II, the state's population has grown dramatically—rapid development that has put the state's environment under great strain. Colorado today is a place where ancient natural wonders mix with a high-tech economy and a diverse, energetic population.

Statehood and Settlement

The late 1860s and 1870s saw tremendous growth and prosperity in the Colorado Territory, much of it brought about by the arrival of the railroads.

The railroads brought thousands of new settlers into the territory. Many

Completed in 1870, the Denver Pacific Railroad ran from Denver to Cheyenne, Wyoming, thus connecting Colorado's capital with the Transcontinental Railroad that linked the East and West coasts. By 1880, narrow-gauge railroads like the one shown in this engraving were making their way through Rocky Mountain passes.

newcomers took advantage of the federal Homestead Act of 1862, which gave 160 acres of land to any family willing to settle on it for at least five years. Others bought land from the railroads themselves—the railroad companies received large grants of government land along their routes, which were then sold to the many families eager to try their luck raising wheat or corn in eastern Colorado.

It did take luck—and plenty of hard work—to successfully farm Colorado's plains. It was a dry region with little rainfall, and settlers had to dig irrigation canals to bring water to their fields. Drought was always the Colorado farmer's biggest worry.

There were other dangers, too. Prairie fires could send walls of flame roaring across dry fields. Huge swarms of grasshoppers sometimes destroyed a farmer's crops in a matter of hours.

The railroads also made Colorado a center of the "beef boom" that swept the West in the 1870s. Cowboys drove herds of longhorn cattle up from Texas to graze on the Colorado grasslands and then sent the fattened steers to market by rail. Many of the great Colorado ranches of this era were financed by companies in the East or in Europe, especially in Britain.

The great era of cattle raising in Colorado lasted little more than a decade. As more farmers arrived on the plains in the 1870s, less land and water was available for cattle. The

brutal winter of 1886–87 also killed hundreds of thousands of cattle in Colorado and across the West in what ranchers called "the great die-off." It took Colorado's ranching industry decades to recover.

But much of Colorado's wealth still came from precious minerals. In 1875, prospectors working near the abandoned gold mines on Clear Creek discovered rich deposits of lead and silver. Once again, fortune hunters by the thousands swarmed into Colorado. Within three years, the population of Leadville, capital of this latest mineral boom, reached 30,000—almost as many people as in Denver.

The lucky ones made huge fortunes, sometimes literally overnight. In one famous incident, a laborer hired to bury a dead prospector struck silver while digging the grave. Forgotten in the excitement that followed, the miner's corpse lay in a snowdrift until spring.

In another incident, a grocer named Horace Tabor loaned a few dollars' worth of supplies to some miners in return for a share in any silver they might find. The miners hit "pay dirt," and Tabor was on his way to a fortune that eventually totaled $9 million.

Tabor spent some of his wealth to build Leadville's amazing opera house. Completed in 1881, the luxurious structure was the largest theater between the Mississippi River and the Pacific Ocean.

Ranchers, farmers, and miners all celebrated when Colorado finally achieved statehood in 1876. Colorado had first applied for statehood in the mid-1860s, but Congress had turned the territory down several times, mostly because the proposed state constitution would have denied the vote to African Americans. This went against the federal civil rights laws passed after the Civil War.

The state constitution was changed, and on August 1, 1876, Colorado joined the Union as the thirty-eighth state. Because statehood came just after the United States celebrated the centennial (hundredth anniversary) of its independence, Colorado was nicknamed the Centennial State.

The late 1870s and early 1880s once again brought warfare between Native Americans and white settlers in Colorado. This time the hunger for mineral riches played an important part in the struggle.

In 1868, Congress had set aside much of the western slope of the Rockies as a reservation for the Ute nation. In the mid-1870s, however, gold was found in the San Juan Range, and white prospectors began to invade the Ute's rugged homeland.

With tensions on the rise, the U.S. government sent journalist Nathan Meeker into Ute territory. Meeker

Joseph Hitchens produced this fanciful painting to celebrate Colorado's 1876 admission to the Union. Beneath a triumphal arch, Jerome Chaffee, territorial secretary and one of the first U.S. senators from Colorado, presents the new state (symbolized by the young woman in white) to a figure representing "Columbia," or the United States.

hoped to keep the peace in Ute country by teaching the Utes to farm. The Utes, however, did not wish to give up their traditional way of life. A frustrated Meeker called in the U.S. Army. Troops rushed to the reservation but arrived too late—the Utes had risen up, killed Meeker and eleven other whites, and taken Meeker's wife and children prisoner.

The rebellious Utes quickly surren-

The movement for woman suffrage (the right of women to vote) in Colorado began slowly in the 1870s. By 1893, organizations like the Colorado Non-Partisan Equal Suffrage Organization had won over enough voters to secure the passage of a woman suffrage amendment to the state constitution. Here, a Denver woman demonstrates for the right to vote.

dered and released their hostages, but Ouray, a Ute chief, knew that the thirst for revenge would be added to the white hunger for gold and land. Ouray made the long trip to Washington, D.C., to plead for fair treatment for his people.

Ouray won the respect of many government officials, but the treaty that followed the "Meeker Massacre" reduced the Utes' vast reservation to a small strip of land in southwestern Colorado and some territory across the border in Utah. Ouray died just before the army forced the Utes onto their new reservation.

The new state's mineral boom continued into the early 1890s, fueled by a major gold strike at Cripple Creek in 1891 and U.S. government policies that kept the price of silver high. In 1893, however, a national economic slump set in, and the price of silver plunged. Many of the people who had become millionaires in the Leadville boom of the 1870s lost their fortunes as quickly as they had made them. Horace Tabor, for example, died broke in a Denver hotel in 1899, just as the state's mineral economy was starting to pick up again.

Colorado women achieved a notable political success in the 1890s. In an 1893 statewide vote, Colorado became the second state to give women the right to vote—nearly twenty-five years before the Nineteenth Amendment to the Constitution guaranteed that right to all American women.

Trouble at the Turn of the Century

Colorado began the 20th century with a population of about 540,000, nearly three times as many people as in 1880. By 1920 the Centennial State's population neared the 1 million mark.

The first decades of the new century were a time of change for Colorado. The frontier era—an era of pioneering homesteaders, cattle kings, and fortune hunters panning for gold in mountain creeks—was now passing into history. The state was evolving and experiencing some terrible growing pains.

This was especially true in the state's mining industry. Fortunes were still being made at Cripple Creek and other sites, but the people making fortunes were mine owners and operators, not lone prospectors. Big corporations now employed thousands of miners to bring ore (mineral-rich soil) to the surface, where machines smelted (processed) it to yield gold, silver, or lead.

At the same time, a less glamorous mineral—coal—became important to Colorado's economy. Starting in the 1880s, large-scale coal mining began in the counties south of the city of Pueblo. That city grew quickly as the coal mines expanded, and with a ready supply of coal—one of the key ingredients for steel—nearby, Pueblo also became the West's center for steelmaking.

Life for Colorado's coal miners was grim. The mines were dangerous places, and accidents claimed many lives; the work was brutally hard and the pay pitifully low. Beginning in the 1890s, labor unions like the Western Federation of Miners (WFM) and the United Mine Workers (UMW) tried to organize Colorado's miners in an effort to force mine owners to im-

Shown here is a United Mine Workers Union (UMW) membership certificate from 1902, one year before a series of strikes rocked Colorado's coal mining regions. Despite the union's efforts, Colorado's mine owners steadfastly refused to recognize the UMW as representative of the workers' interests.

prove pay and to make conditions safer. The mining corporations fought the unions at every step.

The Colorado Fuel and Iron Corporation, better known as the CF&I, was the state's biggest mining corporation and an enemy of the UMW. The CF&I owned not only coal mines and steel plants, but also the communities in which its employees lived. In the CF&I's "company towns," mining families lived in company-owned housing, sent their children to company schools, and bought their food at company stores with CF&I "scrip," certificates paid to the workers instead of regular money. These certificates could only be used at the company store and were worthless elsewhere.

To protest these conditions and to win recognition and an eight-hour work day, the UMW planned a massive strike for the fall of 1913. On September 23 of that year, 10,000 miners and their families left their company houses and walked to Ludlow Station, near the town of Trinidad, where they lived in tents until the strike was over.

The strikers endured a miserable winter at Ludlow. The strike dragged

This photograph shows the burned-out ruins of the strikers' tent city at Ludlow. During the fourteen-hour battle on April 20, 1914, National Guardsmen soaked some tents in kerosene and set them on fire; the smoke from the blazing tents suffocated thirteen women and children.

on and violence broke out between the strikers and mine guards hired by CF&I. Spring came with no end in sight, and Colorado's governor, Elias Ammons, decided to take action.

On April 20, 1914, Colorado National Guard troops arrived at Ludlow and ordered the strikers out of their tent city. When they refused, shooting began and the tents went up in flames. When the smoke cleared, thirteen people lay dead—two women and eleven children. Five strikers and a National Guardsman also lost their lives in the day-long violence.

Like the Sand Creek Massacre a half-century before, the Ludlow Massacre shocked and angered many Americans. The CF&I finally agreed to some of the strikers' demands, but the company still refused to recognize the UMW. Conditions did improve over time, but labor struggles in the mining regions remained a fact of Colorado life for years afterward.

At about the same time as the struggle at Ludlow, agriculture surpassed mining to become the most valuable asset to the state's economy. Farming in Colorado became more diverse, too. Corn and wheat remained the staple crops of the east-

A deer grazes in a meadow in the 400-square-mile Rocky Mountain National Park. Nearly 120,000 people visited the area in 1920, when the Fall River Road made it accessible to cars.

ern plains, but new crops were introduced—sugar beets (usually grown by Mexican and Russian-German immigrants) in the San Luis Valley, fruit on the western slope of the Rockies, and potatoes in the region around Greeley. Ranching of both cattle and sheep also made a comeback.

Both miners and farmers benefited from America's entry into World War I in April 1917. Crop prices rose as demand for food increased, and Colorado mines produced large amounts of molybdenum and vanadium, two metals used in the manufacture of high-quality steel for weapons.

In the years following World War I tourism became a major industry for the state. Colorado had been a favorite destination of sightseers even in the pioneer era, when wealthy Easterners traveled to the territory to admire "the Switzerland of America." Later, people suffering from tuberculosis and other lung diseases came to Colorado hoping the clear, pure mountain air would help them recover.

Colorado's tourist boom began to take off in earnest in the 1920s, when growing numbers of Americans could afford cars and had the time to travel. Many headed to Rocky Mountain National Park, established by Congress in 1915 as the nation's tenth national park.

The Depression and World War II

As the 1920s ended, the Colorado River Compact went into effect. This agreement aimed to end decades of argument between Colorado and six other Western and Southwestern states over the right to use water from the mighty Colorado River for agriculture and industry.

Colorado's government, farmers, and businesspeople had long believed that because the Colorado rose (originated) within its borders, the state was entitled to the greatest share of the river's flow. The states downstream from Colorado felt otherwise. Under the terms of the compact, Colorado agreed to share the river's waters with Arizona, California, Nevada, New Mexico, Utah, and Wyoming, plus the nation of Mexico.

Water rights were important because Colorado's farms and ranches depended on irrigation. "Water is blood in Colorado," said writer John Gunther in the 1930s. "Touch water, and you touch everything." Rainfall in the farming regions of the state is low and unpredictable; without the water provided by the Colorado and other rivers, agriculture—then the biggest part of the state's economy—could not survive.

Water rights were only one of the issues Colorado farmers struggled with in the 1920s. Crop prices had dropped after World War I ended in 1918 and they continued to fall for the rest of the decade. In an effort to make ends meet, farmers plowed more and more of eastern Colorado's grasslands to plant more crops. Unfortunately, this destroyed the tough plains grasses that held the soil together, putting the entire region in danger of erosion (soil loss).

Two events combined to bring economic disaster for Colorado. First, the New York Stock Exchange crash in 1929 touched off a nationwide business depression. The slump hit Colorado, which had more industry than any other Southwestern state, especially hard. Within a few years, thousands of workers in the mines and factories in and around Pueblo, Denver, and other cities found themselves jobless.

Then a period of drought hit the western plains. Starting in 1934 and lasting several years, little or no rain fell. From Oklahoma to the Rockies, winds carried away the overworked soil in dark clouds that blotted out the burning sun. This turned the entire plains region—including eastern Colorado—into a "Dust Bowl."

Many Colorado farm families left the land and headed to the cities in a usually fruitless search for work. Others left the state altogether for Cali-

Buried in dust up to its axles, a broken, abandoned wagon lies in a farm field near Pueblo at the height of the Dust Bowl. About 30,000 farmers left the state during the 1930s and a million acres of farmland were lost.

fornia. Those who could stayed on their land, hoping to ride out the hard times with grim determination—and grim humor. "Part of my farm blew into Kansas today," one farmer said at the height of the Dust Bowl, "so I guess I'll have to pay taxes there, too."

Slow-moving at first, Colorado's government finally took steps to ease the misery across the state in the mid-1930s. To bring in money, the state did all it could to promote Colorado's scenery and tourist attractions to the rest of the country—for example, putting unemployed people to work building roads and ski lodges in the Rockies.

Despite the nationwide economic slump, this tactic worked: By the end of the decade, tourism was a $100 million-a-year business for the state. "The business depression seems to have speeded up the enterprise of the Centennial State," wrote one observer.

Colorado also received aid from the federal government's New Deal programs, including the Civilian Conservation Corps (CCC) and Works Projects Administration (WPA), both of which provided work for thousands of hungry and unemployed Coloradoans. The federal Farm Security Administration (FSA) did much to

help the state's farmers devastated by drought.

With the FSA's assistance, agricultural researchers developed drought-resistant versions of traditional crops like corn and wheat. The state's farmers also began to plant new crops like lettuce, melons, and alfalfa, which were better suited to the soil of the grasslands. The FSA also moved farm families from the drought-ravaged plains to better-watered land on the western slope and replanted eroded farmland with natural grasses.

By 1937, the worst of the drought was over, but neither Colorado's agriculture nor industry recovered completely until the United States entered World War II in 1941. As in World

Colorado's educational institutions also aided the war effort. As part of the National Armament Program, for example, the Colorado School of Mines at Golden used sophisticated machines like the spectrograph to study minerals and metals for use in defense industries. In this 1942 photo, students at the School of Mines receive a lesson in how to use the spectrograph.

War I, the wartime demand for food drove up crop prices, while mines and factories that had been shut down or slowed down for a decade began running double and triple shifts to fulfill orders from the military. Denver alone gained 20,000 jobs thanks to the construction of an important ammunition plant in the city.

In the words of state historian W.

A wartime photograph shows workers at Denver's Mile-High Steel Fabrication Plant rinsing sulfuric acid from steel destined for a West Coast shipyard. The acid was used to "pickle," or smooth, the steel's surface after its passage through the plant.

Storrs Lee, Colorado quickly became ". . . a storehouse of materials needed to flesh out a nation's wartime wants: steel and sugar, wool and molybdenum, lumber and lead, coal, oil, and beef."

Colorado also became home to several important military facilities, including Lowry Air Base near Denver, Fort Carson at Colorado Springs, and Camp Hale, a training center for mountain troops near Leadville. The U.S. Navy even set up an air base, Buckley Field, in Colorado—a state with no coastline.

Denver became an important center for shipbuilding—sections of merchant ships were built in plants in the landlocked city, then transported to shipyards on the West Coast for assembly and launching.

The state also made a great human contribution to the war effort. About 140,000 Colorado men and women—more than one out of ten state residents—served in the armed forces between 1941 and 1945. Close to 3,000 Coloradoans lost their lives in the conflict.

Cold War and High Tech

World War II and its aftermath—the long "cold war" between the United States and its former ally, the Soviet Union—had a great impact on Colorado.

Colorado was already the most heavily industrialized of the Rocky Mountain states when the war began. The factories and plants built during the war years made the state even more of an economic powerhouse. In the early 1900s, agriculture had surpassed minerals to claim the greatest share of the state's economy; in the late 1940s, manufacturing surpassed agriculture as Colorado's greatest source of wealth.

The war also sparked the state's last great rush for mineral wealth. The lure was uranium—a radioactive mineral used for the manufacture of atomic weapons, like the bombs dropped on Japan at the war's end. Before the war, uranium was mined in tiny amounts and used mainly to color glass. When the cold war heated up in the late 1940s, however, the demand for uranium for weapons production shot up.

Once again, fortune hunters rushed to Colorado; this time, their destination was the uranium deposits in the dry, rocky Four Corners region where Colorado, Utah, Arizona, and New Mexico meet. These modern prospec-tors rode jeeps and pickup trucks instead of mules and carried Geiger counters (a device that detects radiation) instead of picks and shovels, but the result was the same as in earlier rushes—a few people made fortunes and most went home broke and disappointed.

The uranium boom lasted from 1948 until the early 1960s, when the U.S. Atomic Energy Commission (AEC), the chief customer for uranium, stopped buying the mineral in large amounts.

The AEC, which oversees both the peaceful and military uses of atomic energy, opened an office in Grand Junction in 1948, built a major plant at Rocky Flats in 1951, and established several more facilities in the state during the 1950s. As Colorado began to play an important role in the Atomic Age, major defense corporations like Honeywell and Johns Manville moved into Colorado. The Martin-Marietta Corporation for example, built a plant at Rocky Flats to manufacture Titan nuclear missiles.

The U.S. military continued to be a major presence in Colorado after World War II. In the late 1940s, the air force, formerly part of the U.S. Army, became a separate service. The air force chose a site just north of Colorado Springs for its service academy, which serves the same function for the air force as West Point does for the army. Work on the $200 million complex began in 1954 and finished four years later.

In 1957, Colorado Springs also became home to NORAD, the North American Air Defense Command, which was in charge of protecting the nation from nuclear attack.

Concerned that a nuclear strike by the Soviet Union might easily knock out facilities located on the East or West coasts, military planners chose Colorado because of its inland location and the protection offered by the Rockies. NORAD took full advantage of this protection by digging a three-story emergency command facility deep within Cheyenne Mountain. This project was completed in 1966.

The bold, modern architectural style of the U.S. Air Force Academy drew both praise and criticism when the complex opened in 1958. Here, cadets stand in front of the Three Faiths Chapel, one of the academy's most famous and striking structures.

For Colorado's agriculture, the early 1950s saw another period of drought—although this time, farmers were better prepared and survived several years of low rainfall without the crippling hardships that were experienced two decades before. Once again, the drought showed the need for improved irrigation for the state's eastern farmlands.

To meet this need, both the state and federal governments undertook several ambitious projects. In 1959, for example, the U.S. Bureau of Reclamation completed the Colorado-Big Thompson project—a combination reservoir-tunnel system to carry water beneath the Rocky Mountains to irrigate a quarter-

Designed to withstand nuclear attack, the NORAD command center in Cheyenne Mountain took $100 million and nearly a decade to build. If the cold war had ever exploded into nuclear conflict, the command center would have taken charge of America's defense.

million acres of farmland in northeastern Colorado.

The postwar growth of Colorado's Front Range cities, especially Denver, also created an increasing demand for water. Moffat Tunnel, originally the first railroad tunnel through the Rockies, began to carry water to the Front Range in the early 1960s, and in 1962 a twenty-three-mile-long tunnel linked Denver with the Dillon Reservoir.

Energy, Tourism, and Environment

Colorado's post-World War II growth was amazing. Between 1945 and 1972, the state's population more than doubled, to about 2.2 million people. During the 1970s alone, Colorado added another million residents—a growth rate of more than 30 percent, or close to three times the national average for the decade.

What attracted so many people to the Centennial State during this quarter-century? For many, it was the promise of jobs with the new "high-tech" companies, like Hewlett-Packard and Kodak, that opened plants in or near Denver and other Front Range cities (cities situated on the eastern range of the Rocky Mountains) in the 1960s and 1970s.

Colorado also became home to many government agencies during this era, providing jobs for military personnel or government workers. The National Center for Atmospheric Research, for example, was established in Boulder in 1961, and so many federal agencies opened offices in Denver that the city is sometimes called "Washington West."

Besides jobs, Colorado's scenery and quality of life proved a powerful lure for many Americans in the decades following World War II. Majestic mountain scenery, clean air, and ex-cellent facilities for camping, hiking, hunting, and fishing all appealed to people from the crowded cities of the East Coast and Midwest.

Keeping pace with Colorado's population growth was a spectacular rise in tourism, which became a $4 billion a year industry by the late 1970s. In 1977 alone, an amazing 9 million people visited Colorado.

Many of these visitors were headed to the state's world-famous ski resorts. Colorado's Rocky Mountain slopes were a favorite of skiers as early as the 1920s, but it wasn't until after World War II that skiing became widely popular as a pastime, and Colorado soon became America's ski capital.

In 1949, Chicago businessman Walter Paepcke turned the run-down western slope mining town of Aspen into a ski resort and cultural center. Other resorts—most notably Crested Butte, Telluride, Steamboat Springs, and Vail—followed later. By the mid-1970s, these resorts were selling close to 7 million lift tickets each year.

The state's terrific growth, however, was not without problems. So many new residents and so many visitors put a great strain on Colorado's

More than ten million skiers sweep down Colorado's slopes each winter. Vail (right) became one of the state's most popular ski areas in the 1970s, joining Aspen, Telluride, Steamboat Springs, and other world-class resorts.

The 1970s and 1980s saw many protests against Colorado's nuclear and chemical warfare facilities. Here, demonstrators form a human chain around the Rockwell Corporation's plant at Rocky Flats. (The plant was closed in the 1980s.)

fragile environment. Smog in Denver and smoke from coal-fired electrical plants, for example, led to the 1966 passage of Colorado's first laws aimed at controlling air and water pollution.

Colorado's atomic and defense industries brought their own share of environmental problems. In the uranium boom of the 1950s, many tons of radioactive ore were used as landfill in Grand Junction and simply dumped in heaps outside of Durango. Concern over the health dangers posed by these materials led to long and expensive clean-ups that began in the 1960s and continue today. Many Coloradoans were also worried about the safety of the Rocky Flats nuclear plant, which experienced a dangerous fire in 1969, and the U.S. Army's Rocky Mountain Arsenal, which housed nerve gas and other deadly chemical weapons.

Growth caused social tensions, too. Most of the growth along the Front Range took place not in Denver or Pueblo, but in the growing rings of suburbs that surround these cities. As big corporations and their employees moved into suburbs like Littleton, downtown areas experienced urban decay and financial problems. This led to worsening conditions for poorer citizens, who were often African American or Hispanic.

Denver and other Colorado cities were spared the riots that hit many other American cities in the 1960s, but a plan to integrate Denver's school system by busing African-American students to mostly white schools caused a bitter controversy in the early 1970s. At the same time, Hispanic leaders like Rudolfo "Corky" Gonzalez urged Colorado's growing Hispanic population to organize to win a greater share of the state's economic and political life.

As the Centennial State prepared to celebrate its own hundredth anniversary in 1976, a terrible natural disaster struck. Swollen by rainstorms, the Big Thompson River overflowed its banks and sent a flash flood crashing through Big Thompson Canyon near Loveland. The disaster, the worst in Colorado's history, claimed 135 lives.

Colorado's economy boomed again in the late 1970s and early 1980s, thanks to the energy crisis that shook the nation when prices for imported oil rose dramatically.

Looking for new sources of energy to replace expensive imported oil, U.S. oil companies began to explore Colorado's vast deposits of shale—a type of rock containing oil. Corporations like Exxon moved into Colorado; so did smaller companies hoping to cash in on the expected boom.

Unfortunately, the boom sputtered out in the early 1980s when worldwide oil prices fell. Because the process by which oil is processed from shale is difficult and expensive, it was no longer profitable for oil companies to continue their shale operations. In the slump that followed, 14,000 people lost their jobs in Denver alone, and it took the city's economy several years to recover.

The son of migrant laborers, Rudolfo "Corky" Gonzalez became a leading activist among Colorado's Hispanic community during the mid-1960s, when he founded the Crusade for Justice. The organization's influence waned after a 1973 confrontation in which a member was killed and several police officers were wounded.

Colorado Today

Colorado's population growth slowed in the 1980s and early 1990s, although its growth rate stayed above the national average. This growth was focused on the 200-mile-long Front Range "corridor," which is home to 80 percent of the state's residents. Because most of the population growth has come from "in-migration" from other parts of the country, only about 40 percent of the state's residents are now native-born Coloradoans.

Denver lagged in growth during the 1980s due to the business slump that followed the "oil bust." The 1990 census found that the city had lost 5 percent of its population during the previous decade, but nearly half the state's residents still live in the Denver-Boulder metropolitan area.

Denver gained its first Hispanic mayor, Federico F. Peña, at the height of the oil crisis in 1983. During his two terms in office, Peña successfully campaigned for the construction of a new airport, Denver International Airport, to ease the burden on Stapleton Airport, which had become one of the nation's busiest. The new airport became a source of controversy, however; it failed to open on time in 1994 when many of its advanced technical systems proved faulty.

Peña's election showed the growing political strength of Colorado's Hispanic community, which now makes

The skyline of Denver, the "Mile-High City," at night, set against the magnificent backdrop of the Rockies. From its modest beginnings as a mining camp, Denver has grown into the economic, cultural, and transportation capital of the Rocky Mountain states.

A Texas-born lawyer and former state legislator, Federico Peña served as Denver's mayor from 1983 until 1991. In 1992, he became secretary of transportation in Bill Clinton's administration.

up 13 percent of the state's population and is concentrated in Denver and in the southern counties. In a controversial political move, however, Colorado's voters amended the state constitution in 1988 to make English the official language of the state.

Peña is just one of several Colorado politicians to attract national attention in recent years. Patricia Schroeder has represented Denver in Congress since 1972, and she made history as the first woman member of the powerful House Armed Services Committee. Gary Hart, senator from 1975 to 1987, was a leading contender for the Democratic presidential nomination in 1988 before a scandal disrupted his campaign. Ben Nighthorse Campbell, a rancher of Cheyenne ancestry, was elected to the House of Representatives in 1986. In 1992 Nighthorse Campbell became the nation's first senator with Native American roots, and in 1995 he made headlines by switching from the Democratic Party to the Republican Party.

Environmental quality remains an important concern to Coloradoans. While much progress has been made since the 1960s, the state still faces major environmental problems. In the mid-1980s, for example, the Environmental Protection Agency (EPA) announced that Denver, encircled by mountain ranges that trap smog at ground level, was the worst major city in the nation for carbon-monoxide pollution. (This is partly due to the fact that car engines produce twice as much carbon monoxide at high altitudes such as Denver's than they do at lower elevations.)

Colorado became the center of a national controversy in November 1992, when voters approved Amendment 2 to the state constitution, which prohibited the passage of laws that gave "protected status" to gay people. The amendment also overturned laws in Aspen and other communities that forbade discrimination against gay people in jobs and housing.

In response, many groups canceled

plans to hold gatherings in Colorado, and many people (including several notable celebrities from the entertainment world) urged a boycott of travel to the state. There were fears that the backlash against Amendment 2 would hurt Colorado's vital tourism industry, but it seems to have had little effect. Amendment 2 has been challenged in court by civil rights activists and its future is uncertain.

Colorado in the 1990s is a state coping with the many changes of the last few decades. High technology and service industries, especially tourism, have replaced mining, farming, and manufacturing as its main sources of wealth. Its population has grown more diverse as hundreds of thousands of new residents have come to live and work in the shadows of its mighty mountains. Every year, millions of visitors come to Colorado to admire its scenery and take advantage of its matchless recreational facilities.

"Because it is such a beautiful place to be," a Colorado businessman said years ago, "Colorado . . . draws people, able people, energetic people, people with the skills or the potential to acquire them." For Colorado, the ability and energy of its people are as rich a resource as the gold and silver that lured fortune hunters to the Rockies more than a century ago.

The awesome scenery of Rocky Mountain National Park reminds visitors and residents alike that Colorado is truly "the place where the miles stand on end."

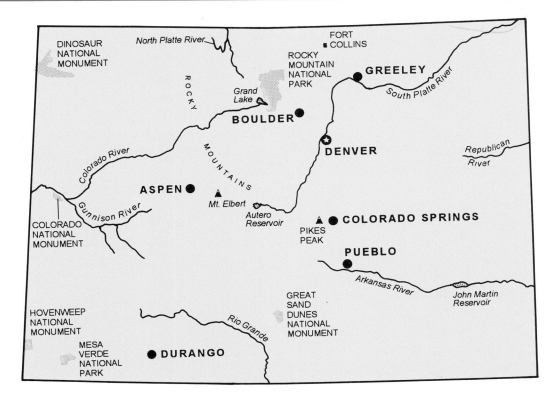

Land area:
> 104,100 square miles, of which 500 are inland water. Ranks 8th in size.

Major rivers:
> The Colorado River system, including the Arkansas, Gunnison, Republican, and South Platte rivers, plus many smaller tributaries; the North Platte; the Rio Grande.

Highest point: Mt. Elbert, 14,433 ft.
> Colorado has highest average elevation (6,800 feet above sea level) of any state.

Major bodies of water:
> Colorado's only major natural lake is Grand Lake, but the state contains almost 2,000 artificial lakes and reservoirs, plus 18 natural hot springs.

Climate:
> Average January temperature: 29.5°F
> Average July temperature: 73°F
>
> Climate varies throughout the state because of differences in elevation.

Population: 3,551,000 (1993)
Rank: 26th
  1950: 1,325,089
  1900: 539,700
  1870: 39,864

Population of major cities (1992):
Denver	467,610
Colorado Springs	281,140
Aurora	222,103
Lakewood	126,481
Pueblo	98,640
Arvada	89,235

Ethnic breakdown by percentage (1993):
White	92.7%
Hispanic	12.9%
African American	4.0%
Asian	1.8%
Native American	0.8%

Economy:
  Manufacturing (metals, machinery, and chemicals); minerals (coal, oil, molybdenum, sand, and gravel); agriculture (sheep, beef, dairy cattle, wheat, corn, sugar beets, and vegetables); tourism; finance; and government services.

State government:
  Legislature: A 2-house legislature, with 35 senators serving 4-year terms and 65 representatives serving 2-year terms.
  Governor: The governor is elected every 4 years and may serve consecutive terms.
  Courts: Supreme court consists of 7 justices who are appointed by the governor but then must be reelected. Other courts include district, appellate, and municipal courts.
State capital: Denver

State Flag

Colorado's state flag features a white band enclosed by two blue bands, symbolizing mountain skies and snows. A red "C", for "Colorado," encloses a gold circle to honor that mineral's role in the state's history. The flag was officially adopted in 1911.

State Seal

The state seal includes miner's tools and mountain peaks; a fasces (the Ancient Roman symbol of justice); the state motto; and the year 1876, the date of Colorado's admission to the Union.

State Motto

Nil sine numine—Latin for "Nothing without Providence (i.e., God's Will)."

State Nickname

The "Centennial State," because Colorado joined the Union in the same year the United States celebrated the 100th anniversary (centennial) of its independence. Also known as the "Rocky Mountain State."

Places

Bear Creek Falls, Telluride

Bent's Old Fort National Historic Site, La Junta

Black American West Museum and Heritage Center, Denver

Boulder Historical Museum, Boulder

Buffalo Bill Museum and Grave Site, Golden

Cave of the Winds, Manitou Springs

Central City Historic District, Central City

Cherry Creek Recreation Area, Denver

Cheyenne Mountain Zoological Park, Colorado Springs

Chimney Rock Archaeological Site, Archuleta County

Colorado National Monument, Fruita

Colorado School of Mines Geology Museum, Golden

Colorado Ski Museum, Vail

Colorado State History Museum, Denver

Curecanti Recreation Area, Montrose

Denver Art Museum, Denver

Dinosaur National Monument, Moffat County

Estes Park Historical Museum, Estes Park

Garden of the Gods, Colorado Springs

Great Sand Dunes National Monument, Alamosa

to See

Gunnison National Monument, Montrose

Hovenweep National Monument, Montezuma County

Larimer Square Historical District, Denver

Lookout Mountain, Golden

Mesa Verde National Park, Cortez

Molly Brown House Museum, Denver

Mount of the Holy Cross, Redcliff

Museum of Natural History, Denver

Museum of Western Art, Denver

Pikes Peak, Colorado Springs

Professional Rodeo Hall of Champions, Colorado Springs

Red Rocks Park Amphitheater, Morrison

Restored Mining Camp, Leadville

Rocky Mountain National Park, Estes Park

Royal Gorge of the Arkansas River, Canon City

San Juan National Forest, Durango

State Capitol, Denver

U.S. Air Force Academy, Colorado Springs

United States Mint, Denver

Will Rogers Memorial, Colorado Springs

Yucca House National Monument, Cortez

State Flower

In 1899, the Rocky Mountain columbine became Colorado's official state flower. This tall wildflower has beautiful two- or three-inch-wide blue and white blossoms.

State Bird

A small white-winged bird common on Colorado's eastern plains, the lark bunting is the official state bird. There were many other candidates for state bird, but the lark bunting won out thanks to a campaign led by a Fort Collins teacher.

State Tree

The Colorado blue spruce, the official state tree, is a magnificent evergreen that can grow to a height of 100 feet. It is covered with small, pointed bluish-gray needles.

Colorado History

A.D. c. 1 Basketmaker Culture established at Mesa Verde

c. 700 Beginning of Pueblo building at Mesa Verde

c. 1300 Pueblo Culture at Mesa Verde experiences mysterious decline

1598 Juan de Oñate becomes first European to reach present-day Colorado

1682 France claims eastern Colorado

1776 Spanish missionaries explore Mesa Verde

1803 Louisiana Purchase transfers much of Colorado region to U.S.; Spain still claims western part

1806 Lt. Zebulon Pike sites (but doesn't climb) Pikes Peak

1819 Western Colorado becomes Mexican territory

1833 Bent's Fort becomes chief white outpost in Colorado region

1848 Mexico gives up western Colorado to U.S. after Mexican-American War

1851 San Luis, Colorado's oldest non-Indian town, established

1858 Gold strike near Pikes Peak draws thousands of fortune seekers • Denver founded

1859-60 Gregory Gulch and Leadville gold rushes

1861 Colorado Territory organized

1864 Sand Creek Massacre

American

1492 Christopher Columbus reaches the New World

1607 Jamestown (Virginia) founded by English colonists

1620 *Mayflower* arrives at Plymouth (Massachusetts)

1754–63 French and Indian War

1765 Parliament passes Stamp Act

1775–83 Revolutionary War

1776 Signing of the Declaration of Independence

1788–90 First congressional elections

1791 Bill of Rights added to U.S. Constitution

1803 Louisiana Purchase

1812–14 War of 1812

1820 Missouri Compromise

1836 Battle of the Alamo, Texas

1846–48 Mexican-American War

1849 California Gold Rush

1860 South Carolina secedes from Union

1861–65 Civil War

1862 Lincoln signs Homestead Act

1863 Emancipation Proclamation

1865 President Lincoln assassinated (April 14)

1865–77 Reconstruction in the South

1866 Civil Rights bill passed

1881 President James Garfield shot (July 2)

History

1896 First Ford automobile is made

1898–99 Spanish-American War

1901 President William McKinley is shot (Sept. 6)

1917 U.S. enters World War I

1922 Nineteenth Amendment passed, giving women the vote

1929 U.S. stock market crash; Great Depression begins

1933 Franklin D. Roosevelt becomes president; begins New Deal

1941 Japanese attack Pearl Harbor (Dec. 7); U.S. enters World War II

1945 U.S. drops atomic bomb on Hiroshima and Nagasaki; Japan surrenders, ending World War II

1963 President Kennedy assassinated (November 22)

1964 Civil Rights Act passed

1965–73 Vietnam War

1968 Martin Luther King, Jr., shot in Memphis (April 4)

1974 President Richard Nixon resigns because of Watergate scandal

1979–81 Hostage crisis in Iran: 52 Americans held captive for 444 days

1989 End of U.S.-Soviet cold war

1991 Gulf War

1993 U.S. signs North American Free Trade Agreement with Canada and Mexico

Colorado History

1868–69 Cheyennes defeated in fighting with U.S. Army

1876 Colorado admitted to the Union (August 1)

1877 Leadville silver strike; start of silver and lead boom

1879–81 Ute Indians driven from western Colorado

1891 Gold found at Cripple Creek

1893 Colorado becomes second state to grant women voting rights

1906 Denver's U.S. Mint begins operation

1914 Several people killed in Ludlow coal miners' strike

1930s Drought and winds turn Colorado's plains into a "dust bowl"

1942 10,000 Japanese Americans forced into internment camps near Grenada

1958 U.S. Air Force Academy at Colorado Springs completed

1965 North American Air Defense Command established in Cheyenne Mountain

1976 Over 100 people killed in flooding along the Big Thompson River

1988 Drought conditions destroy 1 million acres of Colorado land

1992 Amendment 2 approved by Colorado voters

1994 Fourteen firefighters killed battling forest fires

James Beckwourth

James Beckwourth (c.1798–c.1867) This famous African-American scout and fur trader spent many years in the Rocky Mountains. In 1842, he built a trading post which eventually became the city of Pueblo.

Black Kettle (b. ?–1868) Cheyenne chief Black Kettle tried and failed to keep the peace between his people and white Colorado settlers. He survived the 1864 Sand Creek Massacre only to be killed by the U.S. Army at the Washita River in present-day Oklahoma four years later.

William Bent (1809–69) With his brother and other fur traders, Bent built Bent's Fort in 1833, the first major non-Indian outpost in the Colorado region.

John Evans (1814–97) Governor of the Colorado Territory (1852–65), Evans also built the Denver Pacific Railroad and founded the school that became the University of Denver.

Nathan Cook Meeker (1817–79) A journalist and public official, Meeker co-founded the Greeley Community in 1870. His death nine years later at the hands of Ute Indians sparked the last major white-Native American conflict in Colorado.

Ouray (1820–1883) A Ute chief, Ouray tried to preserve his people's lands during the mining boom of the 1870s and 1880s. He died shortly before the Utes were moved to a reservation.

Meyer Guggenheim (1828–1905) Guggenheim made a vast fortune during the Leadville mining boom. He and his sons formed the Philadelphia Smelting and Mining Company, which by the early 1900s was a leading smelting company.

Horace Austin Tabor (1830–99) Born in Vermont, Tabor arrived in Colorado during the 1859 Pike's Peak Gold Rush. He eventually made nearly $10 million, but lost his entire fortune in the 1890s.

Florence Sabin (1871–1953) This Central City-born medical researcher and public-health worker was the first woman elected to the National Academy of Sciences.

Margaret Tobin "Molly" Brown (1873–1932) Denver-native Molly Brown was best known for her colorful lifestyle and for surviving the sinking of the ocean liner *Titanic* in 1912. Her life was the basis for *The Unsinkable Molly Brown*, a popular Broadway musical.

Lon Chaney (1883–1930) This Colorado Springs-born actor terrified silent-movie audiences with his performances in early horror classics like *The Hunchback of Notre Dame* (1923) and *The Phantom of the Opera* (1925).

Douglas Fairbanks (b. Douglas Ulman; 1883–1939) This Denver native became one of the greatest movie stars of the silent film era. His best-remembered films are *The Mark of Zorro* (1920) and *The Thief of Baghdad* (1924).

William H. "Jack" Dempsey (1895–1983) Born in Manassa, Dempsey was world heavyweight boxing champion from 1919 until his defeat by Gene Tunney in 1926.

Paul Whiteman (1890–1967) In the 1920s, this Denver-born bandleader introduced many Americans to jazz through his orchestral arrangements. He also conducted the first performance of George Gershwin's "Rhapsody in Blue" (1927).

Mamie Geneva Doud Eisenhower (1896–1979) Eisenhower, a Denver native, was first lady of the United States from 1953 to 1961.

Mamie Eisenhower

Willard Frank Libby (1908–80) This Grand Valley-born scientist won the 1960 Nobel Prize in Chemistry for his 1947 discovery of radiometric age dating, the first reliable technique for finding the age of fossils and other relics.

Byron Raymond White (b. 1917) White, a native of Fort Collins, won the nickname "Whizzer" as a football player at the University of Colorado. He was appointed U.S. deputy attorney general in 1961 and became an associate justice of the Supreme Court in 1962.

M. (Michael) Scott Carpenter (b. 1925) A U.S. Navy test pilot, Carpenter, a native of Boulder, was one of the original seven *Mercury* astronauts. In 1962 he became the second U.S. astronaut to orbit the earth in the space capsule *Aurora 7*.

Hannah Green (b. 1932) A resident of Golden, Green worked as a teacher of deaf children before writing such well-known novels as *I Never Promised You a Rose Garden* and *The Far Side of Victory*.

Gary Warren Hart (b. 1937) Hart represented Colorado in

the U.S. Senate as a Democrat from 1975 to 1987. Once considered a leading contender for the presidency, his 1988 bid for the White House was frustrated by scandal.

Patricia Schroeder (b. 1940) A lawyer, social activist, and well-known politican, Schroeder has represented Colorado in Congress since 1972; she was the first woman representative to serve on the Congress's Armed Services Committee.

John Denver (John Deutschendorf, Jr.; b. 1943) This folk singer renamed himself to honor his adopted state, which he celebrated in pop hits like "Rocky Mountain High" (1972).

Federico Peña (b. 1947) In 1983, Peña made history as the first Hispanic mayor of Denver. He was appointed secretary of transportation by President Bill Clinton in 1993.

John Elway (b. 1960) Quarterback for the Denver Broncos, Elway led his team to two Super Bowl victories in 1987 and 1988 and earned the NFL's Most Valuable Player award in 1988.

Pictures in this volume:

American Heritage Center, University of Wyoming: 31

Archives, University of Colorado at Boulder Libraries: 48 (CU World Citizens, Box 5, Scrapbook 4)

Boulder Convention and Visitors' Bureau: 2

Courtesy, Colorado Historical Society: 22(top) (neg. F24,285), 22 (bottom), 26-27, 28 (top) (neg. F24,623), 32-33, 49

Denver Metro Convention and Visitors' Bureau: 50-51, 53

Denver Public Library, Western History Department: 34

Dover: 30, 60

Joslyn Art Museum, Omaha, Nebraska: 17

Library of Congress: 7, 11 (top), 12, 15 (top), 15 (bottom), 16, 19, 21, 24, 28 (bottom), 29, 35, 36, 37, 38, 41, 42, 61

Local History Collection, Pikes Peak Library District: 44

Courtesy Museum of New Mexico: 14 (#92063)

National Park Service: 9, 11 (bottom)

Pueblo Library District: 40

U.S. Air Force: 45

U.S. Department of Transportation: 52

Vail Associates: 47 (Jack Affleck)

About the author:

Charles A. Wills is a writer, editor, and consultant specializing in American history. He has written, edited, or contributed to more than thirty books, including many volumes in The Millbrook Press's *American Albums from the Collections of the Library of Congress* series. Wills lives in Dutchess County, New York.

Suggested reading:

Athearn, Robert G., *The Coloradans*, Albuquerque, NM: University of New Mexico Press, 1976

Dannen, Kent, *Colorado: Rocky Mountain Country*, Chicago: Rand McNally, 1983

Downey, Matthew T., *Colorado: Crossroads of the West*, Boulder, CO: Pruett Publishing Co., 1976

Kent, Deborah, *America the Beautiful: Colorado*, Chicago: Childrens Press, 1989

Michener, James A., *Centennial*, New York: Random House, 1974

Sprague, Marshall, *Colorado: A History*, New York: Norton, 1984

For more information contact:

Colorado Historical Society
The Colorado History Museum
1300 Broadway
Denver, CO 80203-2137
Tel. (303) 866-3682

Denver Metro and Convention & Visitors Bureau
225 W. Colfax
Denver, CO 80202
Tel. (303) 892-1112

INDEX

Page numbers in *italics* indicate illustrations